I0990004

Dear Parent:

Congratulations! Your child is taking the first steps on an exciting journey. The destination? Independent reading!

STEP INTO READING® will help your child get there. The program offers five steps to reading success. Each step includes fun stories and colorful art. There are also Step into Reading Sticker Books, Step into Reading Math Readers, Step into Reading Phonics Readers, Step into Reading Write-In Readers, and Step into Reading Phonics Boxed Sets—a complete literacy program with something to interest every child.

Learning to Read, Step by Step!

Ready to Read   Preschool–Kindergarten
• big type and easy words • rhyme and rhythm • picture clues
For children who know the alphabet and are eager to begin reading.

Reading with Help   Preschool–Grade 1
• basic vocabulary • short sentences • simple stories
For children who recognize familiar words and sound out new words with help.

Reading on Your Own   Grades 1–3
• engaging characters • easy-to-follow plots • popular topics
For children who are ready to read on their own.

Reading Paragraphs   Grades 2–3
• challenging vocabulary • short paragraphs • exciting stories
For newly independent readers who read simple sentences with confidence.

Ready for Chapters   Grades 2–4
• chapters • longer paragraphs • full-color art
For children who want to take the plunge into chapter books but still like colorful pictures.

STEP INTO READING® is designed to give every child a successful reading experience. The grade levels are only guides. Children can progress through the steps at their own speed, developing confidence in their reading, no matter what their grade.

Remember, a lifetime love of reading starts with a single step!

For Nancy and Michael Butner,
with love —S.R.R.

To Mom and Dad, thanks! —R.H.

Photograph credit (page 48): © National Media Museum/SSPL

Text copyright © 2012 by Shirley Raye Redmond
Cover art and interior illustrations copyright © 2012 by Red Hansen

Visit us on the Web!
StepIntoReading.com
www.randomhouse.com/kids

Educators and librarians, for a variety of teaching tools, visit us at
www.randomhouse.com/teachers

Library of Congress Cataloging-in-Publication Data
Redmond, Shirley Raye.
Fairies! : a true story / by Shirley Raye Redmond ; illustrated by Red Hansen.
    p.   cm.
ISBN 978-0-375-86561-9 (trade pbk.) — ISBN 978-0-375-96568-5 (lib. bdg.)
1. Fairies—Juvenile literature. I. Hansen, Red, ill. II. Title.
GR549.R43 2012
398.21—dc22
2010030850

Printed in the United States of America
10 9 8 7 6 5 4 3 2 1

STEP INTO READING®

STEP 3

Fairies!
A True Story

by Shirley Raye Redmond

illustrated by Red Hansen

Random House 🏠 New York

Do you believe in fairies?

People around the world
have told stories about fairies
for a long time.
In some stories,
fairies come out to dance
when the moon is full.
Sometimes they steal babies
from their cradles.
They leave fairy children
in their place.

In Ireland,
fairies are called
the wee folk.
In parts of Africa,
there are kind fairies
called azizas (say ah-ZEE-zahz).

The brownies of England
and Scotland are helpful.
They run errands
and clean stables.

But not all fairies are friendly.

Britain's ugly spriggans

bring bad weather to ruin crops.

And the leshy,

or Slavic forest fairies,

beat people with sticks

and tree limbs.

Cautious travelers carried

dry bread in their pockets

to protect themselves

from fairy mischief.

More than two centuries ago,

brothers Jacob and

Wilhelm Grimm

spent many years

collecting German fairy tales.

Their book,

Children's and Household Tales,

was published in 1812.

It became popular

around the world.

But are fairies real?

Today, most people say no.

Some folklore researchers,

though, say maybe.

They say that

a long time ago

in Great Britain

there may have been

a group of small people.

They may have been conquered

by tall invaders.

To avoid capture,

these small people

hid in the forest.

They wore green clothes

so they would be hard to spot.

They came out only at night

to hunt and steal food.

Sometimes they even switched

their sick babies for healthy ones.

Over time,

these small people died off.

But their neighbors

still told tales about them.

There are others
who say fairies are real.
They insist they have seen them!
In 1842,
in Stowmarket, England,
a man saw a dozen fairies
dancing in the moonlight.

He ran home
and told his neighbors.
They rushed back
to the meadow.
But when they got there,
the fairies had disappeared.

William Blake was a famous
British poet.
He claimed to have seen
a fairy funeral.
He told his friends
the fairies were
as small as grasshoppers.
They carried a dead fairy
on a rose petal.
They sang a sad song
as they passed him
in the garden.

Did these men

really see fairies?

Maybe.

Maybe not.

People sometimes make up stories

to explain things

they don't understand.

Weather can play tricks

on our eyes.

Fairies dancing in a meadow

might be nothing more

than fireflies or snowflakes.

Some people who think
they have seen fairies
have been tricked.
The most famous fairy prank
took place
in Cottingley, England.

One afternoon in July 1917,
two cousins named Elsie Wright
and Frances Griffiths
drew some pretty fairy pictures.
They cut them out
like paper dolls.

Elsie took a photo of Frances
talking to the fairies.
Frances took a photo of fairies
dancing in Elsie's lap.

Elsie's father,

Mr. Wright,

developed the photos.

At first,

he was puzzled.

He thought the blurry images

were birds or empty bags.

Elsie told him

that she and Frances

had found fairies in the woods.

Three years later,
Elsie's mother met a man
named Edward Gardner.
He was a well-known teacher
of fairy folklore.
Mrs. Wright told him
that her daughter had
taken photos of fairies.

Mr. Gardner showed the photos
to men at the Kodak camera lab
in London.
One man said
the pictures were fake.
But another man noticed
a blur in a photo.
He said that meant
the fairy was moving.
He said the photos were real!

Mr. Gardner was delighted.
He told everyone he knew
that fairies lived
in Cottingley Woods.
He asked the girls
to take more fairy photos.
They agreed.
They sent three more photos
to Mr. Gardner.

Newspapers reported
the amazing news.
"Fairies in Yorkshire,"
the headlines declared.
"An Epic-Making Event."

Some people laughed.

Others believed

the fairies were real.

They went to Cottingley

to hunt for fairies.

They visited Elsie and Frances.

They asked the girls

to show them where

they had taken the photos.

Sir Arthur Conan Doyle
was a famous author.
He wrote
the Sherlock Holmes
mystery stories.
He believed
Elsie and Frances's
fairies were real.
In 1922,
Sir Arthur wrote
about Frances and Elsie
in a book called
The Coming of the Fairies.

All over England,

people read it.

More and more visitors

went to Cottingley.

The town became famous.

People called it Fairyland.

Many years went by.

In 1981,

when Elsie and Frances

were old women,

they admitted that the

fairy photos were a joke.

"It was just Elsie and I

having a bit of fun,"

Frances said.

"I can't understand to this day

why they were taken in."

Elsie said the fairies

were only paper cutouts

mounted on twigs

with long, sharp hat pins.

This fairy hoax

happened long ago.

But the photos

are still famous.

Recently,

they sold for almost $40,000!

People still go to Cottingley
to look for fairies in the woods.
They still read
the fairy tales written
by the Brothers Grimm.
There are poems and plays
about fairies, too.
Could some of
the old fairy stories be true?
Will a piece of dry bread
protect you
from fairy troublemakers?
What do *you* think?

Author's Note

This is Frances Griffiths
with the fairies drawn
by her cousin Elsie Wright.
The fairies were inspired
by illustrations in the
popular children's book
Princess Mary's Gift Book.
They were drawn on
discarded sandwich-wrap paper.

53100